Rot & Ripening

Rot & Ripening
© Rissa Pappas / Cathexis Northwest Press

No part of this book may be reproduced without written permission
of the publisher or author, except in reviews and articles.

First Printing: 2026

ISBN: 979-8-9928991-4-6

Cover Image by erik cid
Editing & Design by C. M. Tollefson
Cathexis Northwest Press
cathexisnorthwestpress.com

Rot & Ripening

Rissa Pappas

Cathexis Northwest Press

to the good ones

Table Of Contents

The Wastes of Eden	1
Executioner	3
Caretaker	15
Conjurer	27

The Wastes of Eden

Women move through ruins single file
winding under veils of hornet swarms
shimmering the eves of towers crumbling
Imperceptibly they grow old
shoulders and necks drooping
weak stems toward early frost

Healers only ever can intend
with weeds and drams for props
the play played out on platforms
once sacred as cathedrals for old gods
Painted rectangles guide worshippers
along paths like veins toward a heart
that didn't survive

Men before rode in boxes with wheels
Many ride them still in their still way
sockets cupping half shadows
facing north and south

But the women only walk and mostly stop
when one of their kind ceases to rise
and they take each of her limbs
carry her to the nearest water and leave her
draped there on the edge a hand
dangling in for comfort a face
become young in the rippling

Executioner

I lived through it all, but between What Happened and "What now?" was my favorite time.

Before we lost the grids, we ate McMuffins every day. We guzzled soda. Everything strongarmed onto billboards, compressed spectrums of fake flavors, we ate with glee. Once it ran out, the recipe for special sauce would be lost to time.

We waded into penthouses with bloodstained carpets. We dragged $5,000 couches into the streets. Slept among the wildering city pets. Shelled shops ceased to speak of who should go in which haunted dressing room. We wore tuxedos over hiking boots. Dashikis and ballgowns. Diamonds fell out of our go bags and gathered in the creases of curbs.

We coaxed ivy to sprawl. Pulled the grates up and freed the tree roots. Applied color to ourselves and to every surface that asked. Remnants of rage spilling out as joy.

I kept my subway pass long after the trains became boats. The others rained documents of all kinds ripped to ribbons onto the streets. We were done with ink and restrictions. We were done with time being tethered.

The dead we piled in cars in parking garages. Trash was pushed into abandoned buildings. Spray paint dubbed each for easy finding: "Shitty Towers" or "The Garbage Mews."

Time became a swirl just as tightly or loosely wound as we wanted. We gave the days names so we would remember them all. The world finally began to be new. Bullets were becoming a bother. We slept and slept.

Once we realized we could be anywhere we wanted, we went everywhere. Rolled out like battalions in any car with gas, mattresses strapped to roofs. Everywhere standstill traffic—men caught unawares in jams our sister soldiers had created, blockades to corral the herd toward slaughter. Now corpses of cars and men dripped their grease upon the hot asphalt for miles.

We learned to weave through on motorcycles and steer clear of the superhighways. Our days on the road joined the dead cars and dead men in formation like the terracotta army of that Chinese emperor.

This was called by some the Time of Trying or so we heard. The Women's Church of New Beginnings: hastily founded in the North. Razed to the ground thereafter by the Order of Godless Intellect.

"Let's be warlords," said some in the Midwest. And everyone else said, "Go for it. No one cares." And maybe they did. But most of us just kept moving across the land that is ours and nobody's.

A clutch of backbent monks—needling on spindly legs, chicken scratching the crumbling concrete. At first cautious, scrambling to their candled church.

Inside, edges obscured, corners dusted with shadows. Twenty in all if that, clasped each other with the intimacy of occasional lovers. The oldest even seemed like boys. A deepening innocence the old ways would have kept them from.

We weaved our way between and against their speckled arms, foreign touch giving way to groans of old bones guiding hips and knees to the floor. They didn't try to put arms over our shoulders or laugh each other into making us laugh. No sudden moves, not much to say.

We stayed from one new moon to the next. Some of us came away with child, though we didn't know if we could carry them full. The monks prayed us to stay, only a little afraid in the asking. Leaving was mostly easy. Sparing them was harder.

The gun is perfect. With oil, with a bit of care, it can kill forever.

For centuries it made men into apex predators. And then we killed them all. Before years had names, we slunk assured across the lands and through the cities like lionesses. Not much urge to sink into crouch, to stalk, to pounce now.

It used to be a relief to kill—like the cracking of knuckles. Resetting the bones of the world. But the farther we roam, the less we must surround, attack, annihilate.

The prospect of it not being shitty has us spooked. The sky opens and opens. The cult of the gun fades, as do the last of the minds of the old world. How alike our bullets and tears have become. By droplets they disappear into memories.

Without their orders to stay in the sky, many machines have come crying to the ground. Whole constellations abandon the night—angels falling from the house of what we used to call God and now have no use to call anything. Their green hearts were lonely. We understand.

We pick the bones clean and leave them for creatures to shelter in.

The world seems just as loud now, only with different sounds. Raucous murders low in the sky pierce and echo like sirens used to. Sometimes air presses through metal doors or cracked school windows screaming like a mountain lion.

The cats stopped pretending to want us once so many humans were finally gone. They mostly don't attack us. I like to imagine them squeezing into the pyramids, ripping the mummies of ancient royalty to shreds just to make a cozy bed.

We used to be afraid of the many breeds of darkness. Now, we know exactly what isn't in them.

We take care to make only sounds that say, *we are different than before. We are more the same as you.*

The moon is only a skull half-buried in the night sky. Sleeping tulips flecked with blood shift as they dream. Our backs heave as we struggle to pull the air further into our lungs.

Enemies lay in the remnant of a post office lobby, open mouth baring glass teeth to the sky. Ten men in its bloody jaws, darkening the pavement.

The blackred on my comrade's cheeks has reverberated across her face, making a mask of darkness. I wear a beard of blood. Other painted faces loom: our sisters become soldiers one more time.

Our minds and muscles had taken precious time to remember. And my heart has forgotten its joy for killing. It feels like a child's now, bruised by the possibility that over isn't over yet.

On a nearby building, graffiti reads, "Found God. Sent him packing."

The mechanics of the end are here laid bare. Whether or not it's over, I'm through with it.

A new woman is an event. A smile after so many days with only shifting horizons to speak to. Every woman you meet changes your life. Your collision sparks a thousand stars. She is your savior, your angel. Your priestess and lover and soulmate. Mother and sister and daughter. You cherish all of her as she cherishes you. Yes, you, of all people. You are everything to her.

We are not haunted by the ghosts of men. They have been forgotten by the air and so do not move through it. They will be forgotten by the earth once it eats them into carbon. I won't even remember the embarrassment of death upon their sallow faces. We give them to an underworld we will no longer go to.

We are innocenting again. We are kissing and touching sometimes in the evenings. We sing while we walk, silly songs that ghosts wrote that mean nothing now.

Many of us are startled to find out who we really are. How momentum once gathered becomes inevitable. How we all became one generation at once. How we bashed ourselves against the rocks so those to come could reach the shore.

We linger in lands we like, knees bumping, leaning shoulder blades to chests. Each cluster of ruins we come to, I remove all the signs, throw them in a pile. Each town, each street, can be whatever we want now. Or nothing, even.

I will die in the raging wind and be carried away in scavenging angels' beaks, scattered by rooting snouts to speckle the dirt. We will live on in the wild dog and the hookworm. Send us like a message to those who can read it. We will always be here.

Caretaker

My mothers numbered in the dozens
with hair wild and gray.
We lived in husks of houses and other
places that used to be something else.

My mothers saw ashes as opportunities.
Old things could be dusted off and used once more.
My motherborn gathered books.
She made her library in the First National Bank.

"The bank is a collection of voices now,"
she'd say. "The dead never stop speaking."
And so I read, and as I grew older
they told me of things I'd never seen.

At lastmeal one night I claimed my right to roam.
Many of my sisters stood one by one after me.
They declared, too, and we decided to leave
at next full moon. Motherborn came that morning
and took me in her arms. "Listen for us, too.

"We will speak to you every day."
An errant sun pocked the pristine sky.
Cold light filtered through boughs of fir.
At the edge of a great held breath, we began.

I didn't think we would find so much left behind.
But around every riverbank, among every grove
of trees, something jutted out against the landscape
speaking some ugly language we couldn't decipher.

The places built by the dead are also dead.
Wind whistles through their bones. Unrelenting
light warps their faces. Rain beats them a bit more
each year into something it can recognize.

I wished I could bury them. Break them down
and take them away. Maybe all the other things
that are dead and won't decay will migrate there
and pretend to live together.

Someday they will all be gone, and there will be no
evidence of what the old mistaken ones used to believe:
that they were more important than everything else.

We had gone so far and yet the day
our last mother died, we knew.
She told me I would hear if I listened.
I thought of her riverstoned, polished away
into nothing, as I sat beneath the unthinking
trees. Freedom felt frightening now.

The full Buck Moon, echo of expired light, ushered in
Days of Tar. The sky above bubbled black and
cracked with lightning. We couldn't get out from under
the widening cloud threatening to bite down
onto the plains.

"You will always be my daughter," I thought
I heard her say. "Don't worry. You are mine."

In the shadows beneath the shadows, my sisters
fought against the wind.
And then the sky struck down at us
with a hellish wall of sound and swirl of storm,
a tornado touching down to lash the land
and scatter us in the dark.

I felt hands reaching but couldn't hear even
the closest screams. They ran low—scouted
for storm cellars, bunkers, and rabbit burrows.
But I flung my hands at those frightful heavens,
my indignant ache too big for my bones to prop up.

I struck at my belly, beating my hollow drum,
marching into the black.

From under our black blanket, in the silence
of the empty, I began to see paths—
in the air, on the ground, in the streams.
A network of highways whereby birds and fish
and mammals traveled—their great migrations
decrypted.

At nightfall, these travelers followed the light
of a long-dead star. A glaze of glimmer,
refractions smaller than the misty drops
that stipple rainbows into the clouds.
I needed to move with great soldier ant,
great goose, great cutthroat trout
forever swimming.

We must do what our mothers did
but in our own way. Make a better world
for our daughters, even if we never bear
a single child between us. We must unmake.

The broken spine of a bridge protruded
from our resting river, piling up into a dam
of old boats and drowned trees. We must
set it free.

The boats we pulled ashore, left for shelter
and to be eaten by the wind. Water could again
move under the dead bridge, its carcass now
a colony for birds. Once we saw the water flow,
I knew we must do more.

The going grew harder. Vast sameness
pocked with sudden rifts to hidden canyons,
the stitches of the land coming loose over eons.

We followed the sun to bed
and woke with ice in our eyelashes.
Still, we could not escape the mistaken ones.
Nowhere was so lonely that it didn't have
a Bud Light can clacking in the wind.

Ten thousand undying heaps for every
baby born. I wanted to lay down and give
myself up, but that ground wouldn't take me
kindly. We needed new ways to say
the new pain we felt.

New emptiness. We began
to carry birds and mice and other small
frightened things.

We named them—once when they lived,
once when they died, once when they became
bones on a string. They traveled far enough
to shed fear and fur and feathers. Farther
and longer than their little feet and wings
could have carried them alone.

When we find so much trash it might
take years to clear, we settle against
the ground it sits on and listen
to what that ground says. By morning
we decide if it has life enough to save.

We bundle the rubbish to our backs
many feet high and push off in
the direction with the least birds singing.
When the gravel goes gray
we have arrived.

Our loads join the towers of plastic
and dregs that have killed these deadlands
but will take eons themselves to die.

It was years until we found the City of Trees,
a place not built on ruins but on what
was never ruined and only grew more pristine.

Everything was built from what the trees discarded.
Huts curled about the trunks and spiraled upward.
Slender saplings were woven into scaffolds to the sky.

Delicate hands had guided life into shapes most benign.
Mushrooms were cultivated on the corpses
of the fallen and laced into the roots of the living.

The tree sisters welcomed us with a feast.
They were lean and strong, and we
were but walking bones.

They loved our severity, stuck their fingertips
in the hollows of our cheeks. We fell in love with their
round shoulders and thick legs.

We told them about our home and
our mothers and how we extracted detritus
from the ground as we traveled.

They said we were making a trail of purity
across the land. The night became wild with drums
and singing and laughing and moans.

We stayed many named and unnamed days
beneath their speckled canopies, drinking,
feasting, trancing at their fire rites.

When I prepared to leave at last, many of my sisters
didn't want to go. But some young tree sisters wanted to see
what lay beyond the forest, to help unharm the hurt they'd find.

They longed to gather the artifacts of old violences
and destroy all that they could. The others
braided our hair down our backs and we set off.

Parts of birds' nests can never
unspool—synthetic strands so sewn
into our world that to tear them out
would take endless talons.

Microplastics still distend the bellies
of fish. And we breathe them in
like ash from a distant fire.
Perhaps Nature will churn them

gently in her tumblers of air
and water and rock, the particles
grinding fine to dust the world tenderly
with the atoms of unknown ancestors.

Parts per million of you and me.

At last, the sea.
We couldn't know we would be
so long working
to unshackle the world.

What coastline I can see—
only this squint of shoreline will take
the rest of my life to free
from the tangle of past mistakes.

I will become a lighthouse keeper
and this stretch of shore I will protect.
I will keep only what can erode.
I will ride only the horses
that come to me.

Maybe the ocean will notice
my work, and fetch refuse
from miles out and deep
to bring to this shore,

that I might bear it all away, too.
Already, I am gathering
what washes up into my tarp.
Already, my fingers pock

and shrivel. My hair is as gray
as my mother's once was.
I am happy. My body will be
the last wreckage carried away
on the waves.

Conjurer

```
climbing the steps
            the steps
                        the ancestors fought
                                    the ground to build

            all that they made leads
                        up to nothing
            leads me to something that is not there
            leads me to the not there of it

wisdom comes in whispers while I sleep
            in songs    shows a face summoned to the fire
                        sings to circle wide the rot mountains
                        where the world has coughed off
                        its beautiful brown

I need less than I have in me

I climb
            the steps
                        until
                                    what I don't need
                                                becomes the nothing
```

the foretell wisest mother spoke
when I was born — to change the way
              women live

I had ancestors around me   she said
they would give me knowledge

she taught me conjure
and windtrance
and sistersight

but I could not change how the mothers
looked at me
touched me less held me not close   spoke
around me not to me

worship is not love   it is a shadow of love
                that stains the sand

before my first blood came I left them

I don't want to change the way
              we live
I want
to be loved like
sisters should be

there is a place I exalt
for it is the end
of one world
           and the start
              of a different one

---

line clawed across the desert a flat wall

separates the land of the long dead
and the land of nothing eternal

I can step into the nothing
      and walk   and walk   and walk

there are no ancestors there whispering

I stay and eat the silence

but the nothing cannot have me in it for long

            the wind fills my steps with sand

she crosses from light
to the shadow side of the canyon — near disappears
                              behind its border

dark head   thick jaw   an eye with no sister
                    a headwrap tied across its grave

I hold up hands   together
say   sister   I am peaceful

                    slowly her hands match mine
                    together against her wide chest

in the quiet of meal together she pulls her robe aside
shows herself to me — she has something I do not have
                an arm with no hand
                and no elbow
                resting on pillows of flesh

I have heard of this but not seen

        they always bother me
she says
                she pushes her robe back

you want it too   she is asking
lonely eye flickering in fire

she is like me   she moves from coven to coven
                waits to feel a new feeling
I tell her   *the fire is warm*   *come*
                we will seek new sisters   *in the morning*

there are colder nights now and we wear two
                    and three of everything
pitch one tent inside another

mice and waddling beetles   snakes even
curl up against us   hares at our hips
when we sleep

and swirls of flies over us when we wake
black stars in the day sky

I almost miss the ancestors — the air without their words
                        is thinner and clatters more

                but when my love is near
                the dead speak less to me

she wants to follow the pinking sun
she wants to fly straight as the questing birds
not in circles like our friends the buzzards
she dreamed   the questing birds will be our friends
                if we meet them where they are going

the other sisters want to fly with her   and I won't
                        be without her

we gather our tents and bittys
follow the pinking sun to meet the night

many days and heat is meeting us again
and then   new sisters   dozens
spread out from one horizon
                to the other
                a line to their lines

three come to us and the others do not stop
                their work

                they say *welcome sisters*
                      this is the Land of Death
how does it kill

                it has its own sun that burns hotter
                and kills all
                we are building a marker all around it
                to close it in

do you go in

                yes — to give the sun something to eat
                we scavenge the cursed paths to widen
                the pure land to the North

these sisters came from high grasses and wet sands
and mountains and swamps they said
bringing cursed waste to the death sun desert

they tell us to go north and around
they tell us not to come back this way

I ask the ancestors which way to go
I say they have answered me
I say we go the way the other sisters told us

the shells of the great insects our ancestors
used to ride still sleep most buried their big
                            metal brains
                            longest in rotting
                            no feet   no legs

when sun does not blink
we dig under their bodies to hide
and wake when the eye closes
purple arms and ankles and knees
we blend into the night
     wind pushes us along
     the broke open jaw
     of the scrublands
     for days   and days   and days

the land changes from brown
       to yellow like a memory of green
            the air shimmers less glows more
            takes less water from our skin

and then it is *landing bird day*
the land is furry full green
the birds touch down and they are our friends
                       like my love said

I see them first   gleamwhite robes
and closer — they are linkwoven   brown skin showing through
heads hugged with coils of white cloth
twisting with black hair hollow for bitty nests

we embrace   give bones of water
sit them beneath a shadeshift on soft grass

they take off their robes and show us their patterned skin
they lift eyeslit veils   pale faces
                    dark band across the eyes

they pull us to them
        wrap legs around us
        hold us as we hold them
tears streak the dust on all faces

some love each other with their bodies
some with stories
*who else have you seen   the red moon daughters
the ones who arrive after all have gone to sleep*
                    *yes the contraptioners have been here
                    see the watercatchers they built us*

one of them wants to love my woman
she looks at me   I give the sign of no
let her enjoy different
            bodies and hearts
            only when she is done with me

this is not the way of the white robe sisters
this is not the way of any sisters
but my love does not fight with me
she smiles

on dark nights we sing each other songs at fire
on moon nights we gather nectars and squat treefruits

many of these days we call *happiest*
very happy
more happy
laughing
making love until we sleep

we stay some time in the carcass of a great worm
whose trail spreads in front of it and behind it
each segment tinks with strung bones
hung from sisters come and gone

some segments sleep deer   and horses settle
                                shadowside

far down a gulley we can slide for water
stalks of something tall grow hair
                      like ours on top

this place looks like cool morning all day
        feels like a notch   feels like stop
I feel like all the days are this way only for me
and I give them all a secret name — stay

when it is time to go   I will not go
I love the horses   and water   and tall stalk fruits

my love says she will stay with me
she loves me
more than she loves
leaving

we rise to say goodbye
our sisters do not rise
they say they will not wind along the worm trail
they want to stay and no longer leave
                    like us

we will live here   until we live no more

my love and I sleep above the slope
fawns lay between us

In mostly chronological order:

Thank you, Audrey Lorea. The title of Your feature film, *Heaven Is Now*, served as inspiration. Thank you, Dr. Punk, for being my soul cat and my constant companion while I created and worked on this book. Thank you, Mom and Dad, for always cheering me on. Thank you, Anthony Ordile, for your feedback. Thank you, FDU MFA community, for continuing to support me. Thank you, Heather Lang-Cassera and Letisia Cruz, for your encouragement. Thank you, C.M. Tollefson, for your time, dedication, and belief in this work. Thank you, writing and dance communities of which I am honored to be a part, for championing me and my writing. And thank you, reader, for engaging with this book.

Rissa Pappas is a writer, editor, and dancer based in the greater Philadelphia area. She earned her MFA in creative writing from Fairleigh Dickinson University. Rissa was previously a publisher and editor at the now-extinct small press Tolsun Books. She once went "viral" for live-tweeting her period. When she's not doing creative things, she transports sick foxes to rehabilitation (despite their chagrin). Follow her antics at rissapappas.com.

Also Available from Cathexis Northwest Press:

Something To Cry About
by Robert Krantz

Suburban Hermeneutics
by Ian Cappelli

God's Love Is Very Busy
by David Seung

that one time we were almost people
by Christian Czaniecki

Fever Dream/Take Heart
by Valyntina Grenier

The Book of Night & Waking
by Clif Mason

Dead Birds of New Zealand
by Christian Czaniecki

The Weathering of Igneous Rockforms in High-Altitude Riparian Environments
by John Belk

If A Fish
by George Burns

How to Draw a Blank
by Collin Van Son

En Route
by Jesse Wolfe

sky bright psalms
by Temple Cone

Moonbird
by Henry G. Stanton

southern athiest. oh, honey
by d. e. fulford

Bruises, Birthmarks & Other Calamities
by Nadine Klassen

Wanted: Comedy, Addicts
by AR Dugan

They Curve Like Snakes
by David Alexander McFarland

the catalog of daily fears
by Beth Dufford

Shops Close Too Early
by Josh Feit

<u>Vanity Unfair and Other Poems</u>
by Robert Eugene Rubino

<u>Destructive Heresies</u>
by Milo E. Gorgevska

<u>Bodies of Separation</u>
by Chim Sher Ting

<u>The Night with James Dean and Other Prose Poems</u>
by Allison A. deFreese

<u>About Time</u>
by Julie Benesh

<u>Suspended</u>
by Ellen White Rook

<u>The Unempty Spaces Between</u>
by Louis Efron

<u>Quomodo probatur in conflatorio</u>
by Nick Roberts

<u>Suspended</u>
by Ellen White Rook

<u>Call Me Not Ishmael but the Sea</u>
by J. Martin Daughtry

<u>Wild Evolution</u>
by Naomi Leimsider

<u>Coming To Terms</u>
by Peter Sagnella

<u>Acta</u>
by Patrick Wilcox

<u>Honeymoon Shoes</u>
by Valyntina Grenier

<u>Practising Ascending</u>
by Nadine Hitchiner

<u>Home Visit</u>
by Michal Rubin

<u>LA CIUDAD EN TI: THE CITY WITHIN YOU</u>
by Karla Marrufo
Translated from the Spanish by Allison A. deFreese

<u>Resin in the Milky Way</u>
by Amanda Rabaduex

<u>Bone Hunting</u>
by Trinity Catlin

<u>Muskets for the Bear Problem</u>
by Andrew Whitmer

Self-Portraits as a Reddening Sky
by Samuel Gilpin

Desert
by Eric Larsh

Leaving the Religion of Self-Harm
by Bailey Blumenstock

Fractured Symphony
by Andi Myles

La dulzura de los naufragios: The Sweetness of Shipwrecks
by Karla Marrufo
Translated from the Spanish by Allison A. deFreese

Love & Fear
by Henry G. Stanton

Sunlight Later
by Jo Matthews

The Longed For Longer For
by Sibani Sen

Brood
by Kelly Granito

Bleeding Ghosts
by Lara Chamoun

Distilled Spirits: Coffee & Recovery
by Robert Piazza

As Jaguars Dreamed On The Earth's Dark Face
by Clif Mason

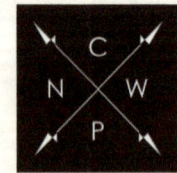

Cathexis Northwest Press